PRUNELLA

OR

LOVE IN A DUTCH GARDEN

PRUNELLA

OR LOVE IN A DUTCH GARDEN
BY LAURENCE HOUSMAN
AND GRANVILLE BARKER

LONDON
SIDGWICK & JACKSON, LTD.
1914

BIBLIOGRAPHICAL NOTE

First Edition, Pott 4to, 1906. Revised and Re-issued, Foolscap 4to, 1911.
Reprinted 1914.

Second Edition, Crown 8vo, 1907. Third Edition, Crown 8vo, reset, 1910.
Reprinted 1911, 1913.

DRAMATIS PERSONÆ

PIERROT.

SCARAMEL, *his Servant.*

HAWK,
KENNEL,
CALLOW,
MOUTH,
DOLL,
ROMP,
TAWDRY,
COQUETTE,
} *Mummers.*

TENOR, *a hired Singer.*

———

PRUNELLA.

PRIM,
PRUDE,
PRIVACY,
} *her Aunts.*

QUEER,
QUAINT,
} *their Servants.*

1ST, 2ND, AND 3RD GARDENER.

BOY.

LOVE, *a Statue.*

PRUNELLA

ACT I

SCENE.—*A garden enclosed by high hedges cut square. To the right a statue of* LOVE, *with viol and bow, stands over a fountain. To the left is a house with prim windows, the centre one projecting over a porch in which hangs a caged canary. The three gardeners are discovered at work, trimming the hedges and nailing up creepers. Behind the further hedge the* BOY'S *voice is heard.*

BOY. O you naughty, naughty birds, now will you
    Come into my garden, and I'll kill you!
1st GAR. Well, what d'you say the weather's going to be?
2nd GAR. Weather ain't up to much, it seems to me.
3rd GAR. It's up to mischief, though:
    Making things grow
    A deal too fast.
    These hedges—since we cut 'em last—
    Don't seem
    As if they know'd as a straight line could mean
    Anything! No; they're all elbows and knees,
    Perking 'emselves about just as they please!
    Oneasy things be trees!

A   1

ACT I BOY. O you naughty little pests, now fly, please!
    Don't come making nests in my trees!

1st GAR. Well, what's to be done now?

2nd GAR. I thought as how—
    While we was on it, gettin' things to shape—
    'T might be a good plan just to give a scrape
    To this old fountain.

3rd GAR.   Ah! you thought that? Well,
    Then don't you do it!

2nd GAR.   Oh! why not?

3rd GAR.   *I tell*
    You—don't you do it! 't's not to be touched, so
    there!

2nd GAR. Well, it can rot then!

3rd GAR.   *You* haven't been here
    So long as I have! if you had you'd know.

2nd GAR. Oh, indeed, oh?   [BOY *throws cap.*
    Now then! now then!

BOY.   Please, Mister Gardener, I
    Was only throwing it at a butterfly!

3rd GAR. Then just you leave the butterflies
    alone:
    They mind their business—and you mind your
    own!
    It's scaring birds is what you've got to do.

BOY. They's scared enough now, mister;—they
    seed you
    Come into the garden.

2

3rd GAR.   Eh? look 'ere, look 'ere!

You keep that sauce for your own chop! D'ye
hear?

Now come and pick this rag up! Don't be slow!

What's coming to the boy now I don't know.

1st GAR. It's just his youth.

3rd GAR.   His *youth!* Hi! Here a minute!

Closer . . . that pocket there . . . what you got
in it?

BOY. Got? What?

3rd GAR.   Why, this. This 'at!

1st GAR.   Lord love yer, look at that!

BOY. 'A picked it up.

3rd GAR.   Picked it up, did you? Where?

BOY. Please, Mr. Gardener, down—down at the fair.

3rd GAR. Oh, so it's the fair you've been to, have
you, then?

BOY. Yes, please, Mr. Gardener, I—went—but I—
I come back agen.

3rd GAR. Who was it told you to go?

BOY.   Please, Mister, I—
I went to see the mummers.

1st GAR.   Mummers? My!

3rd GAR. And you been brought up so respectable,
And b'longing here! What did you go for?

BOY.   Well,—
You see they was going away to-day, some one
told me—

3

And I just couldn't 'elp it!   I just 'ad to see
If they was like—like what I 'd thought they'd be.
An' oh, they was, they was and more so!   There
Was a lot of 'orses and ponies, all polished-shinin',
    just like my 'air
Of a Sunday; an' acrobats, pink-in-the-skin, an'
    clowns
All tumbling about: and ladies, oh!—what had
    gowns
Too short for their legs! and, my word, didn't they
    kick!
And there was a lot of fiddlers fiddling so quick
You couldn't stop to breathe for listening; and
    fairies with wings,
And folk what had sugar-plum things
Stuck all over them!   Oh, and they played
The fool to the life!

1st GAR. Did they now—did they?

3rd GAR.   Well?

BOY. Made you feel you wished you was silly yourself—like as you was ever so.

3rd GAR. Well?

BOY.   Then—then I come away.

3rd GAR. Then, now you

                [*Points him back to his work.*

BOY. Yes, Mister Gardener.

3rd GAR.   Head Gardener.

BOY. 'Ead Gardener.

1st Gar. Oh, I 've seed life in my time too !

3rd Gar. Yes. An' you just encourage that boy.

1st Gar.   *I* do ?

3rd Gar. I 'm feared at 'eart you 're unregenerate, Jeremy !

2nd Gar.   Ah ! what was you up by the gate
So long about this morning ?

1st Gar.   I ?

2nd Gar.   —If not
To see them mummers pass ; more 'n one lot
Went by wi' a band just about breakfast-time.

1st Gar. Ay, so they did.

2nd Gar.   And you there ?

1st Gar.   Eh ! Well, I 'm
Fond of a bit of music and a game.

3rd Gar. What, at your age ? O Jeremy, think shame
Of harbouring of such thoughts !

2nd Gar. [*Sniffing.*]   Ah, ha !

3rd Gar.   Well ?
What are ye up to there, my Samuel ?
What 's come on you ?

2nd Gar.   There 's summat I can smell
The shape of here !

3rd Gar.   What sort of shape 'll it be ?

2nd Gar. Our dinner ! Pigs'-pudding !

3rd Gar.   Good !

ACT I 1st GAR. Ay! though for me—
I prefer chitterlings.

3rd GAR. Ah! I don't know!
I dunno. Chitterlings *in* their place don't go
So bad; but if you was to ask me straight
What I'd have first, if it should be my fate
To die to-morrow, why I think I'd most
Choose tripe and onions!

1st GAR. Peter, add a roast
Potato, and I'm with you!

BOY. Please, misters, say
Ain't 'am and eggs your notion of heaven?

3rd GAR. Eh?
My notion is you'd better get on away
Back to your work—wasting your time all day
Listening to what's not meant for your ears!

2nd GAR. Well,
That talk's made me feel sorry for mysel'—
Hungry. How goes the time?

3rd GAR. It ain't nigh twelve.
Not yet. [*Sighs.*

Enter QUEER, *carrying small table.*

2nd GAR. Oh, good-morning, ma'am,—miss, I should
say.

QUEER. No, you shouldn't: you should wait till
you're spoken to!

3rd GAR. Quite right, Mrs. Queer! Patcher, learn
your place!

6

PRUNELLA

QUEER. I didn't ask *you* to speak!

3rd GAR. You did not, Mrs. Queer, but the sweet-
ness of your looks tempted me to hutter a
hobservation.

QUEER. Ha!

      [QUEER *arranges things, and exit abruptly.*

2nd GAR. What's put her out?

3rd GAR.   Thought of old times, maybe!

2nd GAR. Eh, but she needn't vent it off on me.

1st GAR. Here! did she have
   Her disappointments ever?

3rd GAR.   I don't know.
   I don't know.

2nd GAR.   Ah, you've your suspicions, though!

1st GAR. When did it happen?

3rd GAR. If it did happen—and I don't say so—
   But yet I don't say no—'twas at the time
   When that French gentleman-gardener come
     along,—
   Him as put up that fountain. It was then
   As most things happened that ever happened
     here.

1st GAR. Oh, ho, so that's how it come? What
   does it mean?

2nd GAR. That stands for Cupid. Cupid's the
   French for love.

          Re-enter QUEER.

QUEER. In a few minutes' time your mistresses

7

ACT I   Are coming to sit here: and they 'll expect
Quiet and no disturbance while Miss Prunella
Is doing her lessons.   Mister Gardeners,
You had better *begin* to work! it 's getting late!

                                  [Exit.

3rd GAR. Ah, she don't like our looking at this here
. . . No . . .
Yes, as I say, 'twas that French artist chap—
'Gardener architect' as he called hisself—
Who put that up.   Well,—it was never any
Affair of mine.

1st GAR.   And what else did he do?

3rd GAR. Well,—we don't make a boast of it, you
see,—
But it was 'e
Run off with the youngest of 'em—Miss what 's
'er-name?
—With Miss Prunella's mother, as she *became.*

1st GAR. O-oh! Was Miss Prunella his daughter,
then?

3rd GAR. I don't know.

2nd GAR.   What—didn't they marry when—
When—-er—

3rd GAR.   I *dunno.*

1st GAR.   Come, out with it, man!
What *do* you know?

3rd GAR.   Well, twenty years ago,
That Frenchman, he come here; and he began

Chopping and changing, doing things on his own— ACT I
Improving what he'd better have left alone,
If you ask me. 'Twas he put on the shelf
That graven-image o' Cupid—carved it himself:
And—Miss—Priscilla——

2nd GAR.   Ah!

3rd GAR.   She used to come
And watch him at it.

1st GAR.   Oh! so that was how!

3rd GAR. Ah! that was it.   Then she grows pale
    and thin,
And melancholy-like;—you know the way
That sort of thing takes people—walked about
With a book in her hand, holding it upside down
Pretending to be reading of it—watching him.

2nd GAR. And he a-watching her?

3rd GAR.   Ay, ay!   Before
He made the sign, she was in love with him,
And just as full of it as any goose
Is with the stuffing.

1st GAR. Did nobody find out?

3rd GAR. Ah, p'r'aps Miss Privacy knew—
Or guessed: but she was soft—she didn't say
Anything to the others.   And then, one day,
Just when the statue was finished—she and him—
Miss Priscy and her Frenchman-architect—
Took and run off together.   No one knows
What happened after that.

9

ACT I 2nd GAR.   Well, they must know
    Something: or where does Miss Prunella come in?
3rd GAR.   She come
    Just a year afterwards, as small and young
    As they make 'em—found lying at the door
    Tied up in black ribbon, with a letter written
    By Miss Priscilla just before she died,
    Saying the child was hers.   But more than that
    I don't know, I don't know.
2nd GAR. Well, a poor business that was to be
    sure!
    And what for, eh ? for love !—Cupidity !
    'Stupidity' *I* call it.   I love my love
    With a D—I want my dinner !
1st GAR. So that's where Miss Prunella gets her
    ways,
    Is it? Why, there! I've seen her hanging
    round
    That fountain by the *h*our, all sad and pale
    And star-gazing at nothing :—just as you say
    Her mother used to do.
3rd GAR.   Oh, ay ! she's like
    Her mother : a deal too like her to please me.
    If we don't look out, she'll go falling in love
    With the first pretty fellow she sets eyes upon ;
    And then the deuce to pay !
BOY. Please, Mister Gardener, I saw Miss Prunella
    looking at *me* yesterday—the saddest, sorrowfullest
    10

look you ever saw. It made me blush all down ACT I
into my clothes. Oh! [*Breaks off.*

Enter PRUNELLA. *She is studying a book and
carrying a satchel of work on her arm.
Occasionally she half closes the book, and raises
her head to mutter a piece off by heart; then
halts and looks down again.* 1st *and* 2nd
GARDENERS *go round hedge.*

Oh, hark, naughty birds, what I 'll do t' you;
Go out of my garden, or I 'll shoot you!

PRUNELLA [*Repeating each line twice over*].—
Not to allow my thoughts to stray—
Not to allow my thoughts to stray
Beyond the duties of each day—
Beyond the duties of each day:
Thus only can I hope to be—
Thus only can I hope to be
A type of maiden modesty—
A type of maiden modesty.
Now I know that.

3rd GAR. Hem!

PRUNELLA. What are you doing there?

3rd GAR. Giving Nature a lesson, miss.

PRUNELLA. What are you teaching her?

3rd GAR. To keep straight! I 'll let her know who's
master while *I*'m here.

PRUNELLA. And if you didn't, what would happen?

ACT I 3rd GAR. Why, she'd kick over the traces and be off her own way in no time. She's bad enough as it is, always getting herself [*clips*] out of shape, and trying to be different to what you make her. [*Clips.*] Well, that you can't help, you've just got to come along and put it right. [*Clips.*] First she'll run to leaf—that you can't help—then she'll run to seed—that you can't help—then she goes stalky [*clips*] rots herself—dies and stinks. None of it you can't help.

PRUNELLA. What can you do, then?

3rd GAR. Oh, you—you—can make things uncomfortable for her; you can show her what she ought to be, and keep her in her place—make her toe the line. That's what a garden's for, that's where gardening comes in.

PRUNELLA. Oh dear! here are my aunts already!

3rd GAR. Yes, miss.

PRUNELLA. Lessons! I'm sure I'm growing too old for lessons.

3rd GAR. No, miss—no one grows too old for lessons.

Enter PRIM, PRIVACY, *and* PRUDE, *followed by* QUEER *and* QUAINT. *The* GARDENERS *retire behind hedge, and commence to work.*

PRIM. Prunella, it is lesson-time. Are all your lessons learned?

12

PRUNELLA. Yes, Aunt Prim.

PRIVACY. Quaint, is the outer gate shut?

QUAINT. Yes, ma'am.

     [PRUNELLA *stands apart, conning her lesson.*

PRUDE. Indeed, I hope so; to-day it's very necessary. You had better double-lock it, and draw down *all* the blinds looking towards the road.

PRUNELLA. Why, Aunt Prue, people will think there's some one dead in the house!

PRUDE. They had better do so, Prunella, if it will induce them to moderate their conduct while passing our premises. I have already beheld more than I care to recount to you.

PRIVACY. I heard a disturbance outside.

PRUNELLA [*Leaning forward with a little curiosity*]. Oh, yes——

PRIM. Prunella, deport yourself!

PRIVACY [*To* QUAINT]. You had better bring me the key of the gate.

QUAINT. Yes, ma'am. [*Exit.*

PRIM [*To* QUEER]. To-day we shall not be at home to any one.

PRUDE. Who will call? No one can venture into the streets.

PRUNELLA. Why can't they, Aunt Prude?

PRUDE. Never mind, Prunella!

PRIM. Tell the gardeners to see that nobody intrudes. [*Exit* QUEER.

ACT I BOY O you naughty, naughty birds, now will you
Come into my garden, and I'll kill you!

> [QUAINT *returns with the key, and exit into house.*
> PRUNELLA *wanders toward the hedge.*

PRIM. Prunella, get your needlework,
And bring your little chair:
Assume the task you wish to shirk,
And come and sit down here!

GARDENERS [*Looking round hedge*].
And go and sit down there!

PRUDE. But please to do it decently,
No, do not cross your feet;
These habits have come recently.
Correct them, I entreat!

GARDENERS [*As before*].
Correct them, we entreat!

PRIVACY. Count ten before you say a thing,
Think of each word you use,
Be careful how you weigh a thing,
And mind your P's and Q's.

GARDENERS. And mind your——

> [*Clock strikes 'Cuckoo' twelve times. The*
> GARDENERS *stop speaking and begin to
> count on their fingers and feet.*

BOY [*Behind hedge*]. O you naughty, naughty
birds; now—oof! . . .   [*A dinner-bell is heard.*
3rd GAR. Dinner!

14

PRUNELLA

2nd GAR. Dinner!

1st GAR. Dinner!   [*Boy runs past.*

2nd GAR. That boy gone—forward as usual!

                   [*Exeunt.*

PRUDE. Prunella, regulate yourself!

PRIM. It is time to begin lessons. Have you learned
     your verses?   [PRUNELLA *hands the book.*
     You had better stand while you recite.

PRUNELLA. What is my task to-day?   Behold
     The dawn arises decked in gold;
     Bird, beast, and fish awake to run
     Their daily rounds beneath the sun.
     Shall I alone neglect to ask
     The frightful question, 'What's my——

PRIM. *Vital* question.

PRUNELLA. Shall I alone neglect to ask
     The vital question, 'What's my task?'
     Ah, no! the Power which placed me here,
     Directs me still to persevere;
     To find, removed from dust and heat,
     Materials for a life complete,
     And to pursue with taste subdued
     The gentle paths of rectitude;
     To keep my temper well controlled,
     To be content—do as I'm told,
     Not to allow——

PRUDE. Prunella, retreat the sash!

PRIM. 'Not to allow'—continue, Prunella!

ACT I PRUNELLA. Not to allow . . .
> To keep my temper well controlled
> To be content—do as I'm told,
> Not to allow——
> Oh, I've forgotten it all now! Retreating the
> sash put it all out of my head.

PRIM. You must learn it again.

PRIVACY. Prunella, I have not known this happen
before! You had better carry the book indoors.
Bring *The Gentle Reader* with you when you
return.   [*Exit* PRUNELLA.

PRIM. Do you think she has noticed anything?

PRIVACY. Seen anything? Oh, I hope not.

PRUDE. I think it possible.

PRIVACY. I fancy the fair must be breaking up to-
day.

PRUDE. Three or four bodies of the rabble have
already passed along the road.

PRIM. *Our* road?

PRUDE. I heard—I almost saw them. I'm sure it
is a death-trap to any young girl's modesty to
look out of window while such characters are
abroad.

PRIM. Hadn't we better all go indoors? We are
too close to the road here.

PRUDE. But we must be careful not to be abrupt or
to seem purposeless.

PRUDE. If we made any sudden move, Prunella's ACT I curiosity might be aroused.

PRIM. I think it is aroused already.

PRUDE. Well, she certainly showed a peculiar intelligence about the blinds. She seemed to me to wish to have them up.

[PRUNELLA *returns from the house.*

PRIVACY. Hush! here she comes.

PRIM. I observe a strange agitation in her manner.

PRUDE. She's concealing something.

[*The* Mummers' *music in the distance.*

PRIM. Privacy—there are the mummers again!

PRIVACY. Dear me! But quite in the distance.

PRIM. But she'll hear them—she must——

PRUDE. She's taking notice—she's taking notice!

PRIVACY. Oh, distract her attention!

PRIM. How?

PRUDE. Make conversation!

PRIM. Ah!—it's the gardeners' dinner-hour——

PRIVACY. They will have finished soon.

PRUDE. It looks as if there'd be a shower
This afternoon.

PRIM. I hope you put away your books?

PRUNELLA. Yes.

PRIM.   Closed the drawer again?

PRUNELLA. Yes.

PRIM.   Quite sure?

PRUNELLA.   Yes.

B   17

ACT I PRUDE.   It really looks
   As if there would be rain.

PRIM. Prunella, *do not cross your feet*,
   Don't turn them so much out!

PRUDE. Really I *do* think from the heat
   Thunder must be about.

                        [A slight pause.

PRIM. Ah! They have passed by.

PRIVACY. Dear child, she has noticed nothing.

PRUDE. Innocence is a beautiful thing, Privacy.

                       *[*PRIM *yawns.*

PRUDE. Really, Prim!

PRIM. I am sorry—I think it is more nervousness
   than fatigue.

PRUDE. Reading, Prunella!—Open your *Gentle
   Reader.* Turn to 'The Moon.' No—no, Prunella
   —do not waste your energy in turning pages.
   Discover the whereabouts of the passage by means
   of the Index—placed in the book for that purpose.

                   *[*PRIVACY *yawns.*

PRUDE. Oh, Privacy!

PRIVACY. I beg your pardon.

PRUDE [*To* PRUNELLA]. Have you found 'The
   Moon'?

PRUNELLA. Yes, Aunt.

PRUDE. Then begin. Read slowly and sit straight.
   [*She starts a yawn, but checks it.*] No—'twas not
   yawning.

18

PRUNELLA. 'The Moon.' To-day, gentle reader, we ACT I
will look at the moon, in order to consider its
character, its condition, and its constituents, so far
as they are known. The moon is much larger
than the uninstructed would suppose; it is nearly
a quarter of a million miles away from our globe,
which will give you some idea of its size. Thus
the fastest crow would take nearly four years to
fly from here to the moon, without any pause for
refreshment by the way, and the kingly eagle
would not accomplish the task under three. Let
facts like these, gentle reader, stir your wonder at
Creation's mighty plan, and stimulate modesty at
your own exceeding insignificance.

PRUDE. 'Modesty,' Prunella; you had better make a
note.

PRUNELLA [*Makes a note*]. The moon has from
time immemorial been the subject of foolish
fables, all of which are untrue. The fact that the
contours of its surface somewhat resemble the
human countenance has given rise to an ignorant
superstition that the moon contains a man.
Gentle reader, there is no man in the moon, nor
is it in the least probable that any form of life
can exist there. It is true that the moon presents
to our eyes only one-half of its surface; no one
has ever seen the further side of the moon.

PRIM. Prunella, why do you stop reading?

ACT I **PRUNELLA.** No one has ever seen the further side of the moon! It is probably just the same in all respects as the one we know. [*The* Aunts *begin to nod.*] The moon completes the circuit of the earth once in every lunar month. If uninfluenced by superior gravity the moon, once started, would have gone on in a straight line for ever; any change that has come about is proportional to the earth's attraction, and lies in the direction of that attraction. [*Distant music comes nearer;* PRUNELLA *stops to listen and goes on again. The* Aunts *sleep.*] The earth influences the moon, attracting it by its superior gravity. Once it formed a part of the earth, but breaking away, it chose a course of its own and lost all its heat and vitality. The moon may, therefore, fitly be held up as an object-lesson to all young people. It once committed a rash act for which it is now paying the penalty.

> [*Music again comes nearer; on the other side of the hedge are voices and laughter.* PRUNELLA *stops to listen. Over the hedge a shower of confetti falls upon the sleeping* Aunts. PRUNELLA *turns in timid alarm. Outside a toy bugle is blown on two notes rather like a cuckoo, and a drum is banged.*]

PRUDE [*Awakening*]. What was that noise?

PRUNELLA. I don't know. [*More noise without.*

Prim. Oh! oh! Those dreadful people!

Enter Queer *and* Quaint, *running.*

Queer *and* Quaint. O ma'am, ma'am, ma'am!
The mummers are going by! They 've been
throwing up at the windows and knocking at
the gate, and there are lots more of them coming
up the road.

Privacy. Come, let us go in at once.

Prim. We must retire.

Prude. Queer, Quaint, bring in the chairs!

Privacy. Prunella, my dear, don't sit so! Get up!

[Prunella *gets up all in a dream; her lap is
full of needlework, thimbles, scissors, etc.,
which fall upon the ground.*

Prim. Tut! tut! what carelessness! Gather them
up quickly, and come!

[*Another blast outside.*

Prude. Oh-h-h! [*Runs.*] [*Exeunt the* Aunts.

[Queer *and* Quaint *pick up the chairs.*

Queer. What are you going to do?

Quaint. I 'm going to pull down the top-floor
blinds. I won't have people looking into *my*
room.

Queer [*With understanding of what opportunity a
top window affords*]. Ah! And I believe my window is open. Ignorance ain't innocence; it 's well
to know these things—then you can avoid 'em.

21

ACT I PRIVACY [*Returning*]. Prunella, I have dropped the gate key. Find it and bring it in. Then retire to your room and stay there till you are sent for.

> [*Exit* PRIVACY. PRUNELLA *prepares to follow, takes up the key, then after a moment's hesitation gets on her stool and looks over the hedge. Through the bottom of the hedge creeps* PIERROT. *Half-way through he stops.*

PIERROT. Cuckoo!

> [PRUNELLA *looks down and sees him. There is a long pause.*

PRUNELLA. Was it you made that noise just now?

PIERROT [*Nodding and smiling at her*]. Nice noise, wasn't it?

> [PRUNELLA *shakes her head very seriously. He comes right through the hedge.*

PRUNELLA [*Scared*]. Naughty white boy, you must go away!

PIERROT. No, pretty Dutch doll, let me stay!

PRUNELLA. You mustn't call me names.

PIERROT. You called *me* names.

PRUNELLA. I didn't.

PIERROT. You did—a horrid, nasty name.

PRUNELLA [*Approaching him, half fascinated*]. Tell me—what in the world are you?

PIERROT [*Going on his knees in a mock attitude of prayer and talking very fast, as if in a great hurry to tell his tale and get pardon for intruding*]. Oh,

22

I'm nothing: I'm nothing in the world but a
poor Pierrot. I'm an orphan, I haven't got a
home, I haven't got a friend, I haven't got a leg
to stand on, I haven't got a bed to sleep in, I
haven't had a bit to eat, and I haven't had a drop
to drink for three whole hours. [*Changing his
manner, seeing that he has made an impression on
her.*] There, now you know all about me,—as
much as I know myself, almost. Oh, I'm so giddy,
I can't stand. If you don't look sweet at me, I
shall be dead in a minute.

PRUNELLA. But how did you come here? Who are
you?

PIERROT. Dropped like a bird. I'm the man in the
moon.

PRUNELLA. Don't be silly. There's no man in the
moon. I've been taught that.

PIERROT. Ah! Don't you believe all the things
you're told!

PRUNELLA. But that's in a book.

PIERROT. Never read books. I never do.

PRUNELLA. Don't you learn things?

PIERROT. I know all that's worth knowing. And
now I'll tell you something. [*Draws nearer and
looks into her eyes while he points to himself.*] The
moon has a round face, two eyes, a nose, and a
mouth. That's science. You thought I didn't
exist; but—I've come true. That often happens.

23

ACT I PRUNELLA. But *why* did you come here at all?

PIERROT. Looked at you through the hedge till my heart beat a hole in it! Now I've lost it.

PRUNELLA. What?

PIERROT. My heart.

PRUNELLA. How?

PIERROT. Flown! Up into that tree, just over your head. Can't you hear it crying 'Sweet, sweet, sweet!'—like a hungry bird, eh? Throw it a crumb! Throw it a crumb! There! did you hear that?

PRUNELLA [*Shaking her head incredulously*]. Why don't you call it back again?

PIERROT. Ah! it won't come to my calling—not now! But if you were to call, if you were to say, 'Sweetheart, sweetheart, come!' why, I shouldn't wonder——

PRUNELLA. Oh, you oughtn't to be here, you must go away!

PIERROT. Why must I?

PRUNELLA. Because nobody like you ever comes here.

PIERROT. Would you like them to come?

PRUNELLA. Them! Is there any one else like you in the world?

PIERROT. One or two. You don't believe it? I'm flattered. But truth before all things. I'll prove it. [*Whistles.*] Scaramel! Scaramel! But not

24

quite like me—we are rather a mixed lot, we ACT I aren't all as white as we are painted.

Enter SCARAMEL.

Here is one, now! My man Scaramel. Do you not see the likeness?

SCARAMEL. At your service, if it's my master's.

PRUNELLA. What does he mean by that?

PIERROT. That's his creed—it's what he lives by.

PRUNELLA. He's not like you at all. I don't like him.

PIERROT. But that's rather foolish.   For if every one were just like me, you'd see too much of me, then.

SCARAMEL. Master, she's very young.

PIERROT. Well?

SCARAMEL. Otherwise charming as usual.

PRUNELLA. Oh, please send him away! If you will send him away you may stay,—just for a little.

PIERROT. What's that you have in your hand?

PRUNELLA. A key.

PIERROT. It's a very pretty key. May I look at it? Keys fascinate me. I like to guess what they open.

PRUNELLA. Oh, yes.   *[Hands him the key.*

PIERROT. Now this isn't a watch key.

SCARAMEL. Nor a bed key.

PIERROT. It's not a small key.

SCARAMEL. No; it's a large key.

ACT I PRUNELLA. It's the key of the garden gate.

PIERROT. Is it really? Scaramel, this is the key of the garden gate. Well, a gate has its uses, eh, Scaramel? Ah!

[SCARAMEL *runs off with the key.*

PRUNELLA. Thank you for sending him off.

PIERROT. Don't mention it, pray.

PRUNELLA. But what have you done with the key?

PIERROT. Didn't you see me put it down my back to prevent my nose bleeding.

PRUNELLA. Was your nose bleeding?

PIERROT. Child, child, I said to *prevent* it bleeding. Let us talk of something else. I don't like this place. It's too straight. I don't like it.

PRUNELLA. It's my home.

PIERROT. Do you love it?

PRUNELLA. Why—yes.

PIERROT. Why has your house shut its eyes? That's wilfully foolish. Now I'll tell you a story about a house I once knew—very like this.

PRUNELLA. Really like this?

PIERROT. Where somebody lived very like you.

PRUNELLA. Some one like me?

PIERROT. Asleep, on the edge of a town
　　Where the high-road ran by,
　Stood a house with the blinds all drawn down,
　　As if waiting to die.

26

And everything there was so straight
  With high walls all about!
And a notice was up at the gate,
  That told Love to keep out.

But Love cannot read,—he is blind;
  So he came there one day
And knocked; but the house was unkind,
  It turned him away!

But lo, when the gates were all closed,
  When the windows were fast,
At night while the householders dozed,
  Love entered at last.

PRUNELLA. Oh, you recite quite nicely, better than
  I do. [*Peals of laughter are heard outside and cries
        of* 'PIERROT! PIERROT! PIERROT!' *which
        come nearer.*

PIERROT. Thank you, but I have a deal of practice.
PRUNELLA. Oh, listen! What's this?
PIERROT. Friends of mine.
  Here they come,
  Look at 'em:
  Rollicking, rackety!

  Enter KENNEL, CALLOW, MOUTH, HAWK.
ALL FOUR. Here we come,
  Look at us:
  Rollicking, rackety!
KENNEL. Kennel!

ACT I CALLOW. Callow!
MOUTH. Mouth!
HAWK. Hawk!

Enter SCARAMEL.

PIERROT. Scaramel, good—you're an excellent
servant.
KENNEL and CALLOW. Tawdry and Doll.

Enter TAWDRY *and* DOLL.

SCARAMEL. Here they are, pretty dears.
TAWDRY and DOLL. Here we are, pretty dears.
MOUTH and HAWK. Romp and Coquette!

Enter ROMP *and* COQUETTE.

ROMP and COQUETTE. Last through the gate.
PIERROT. Dance round me!
MOUTH. Jump, little Tawdry, Jump so high!
DOLL. Here's a fine garden.
HAWK. Let's pull it to pieces.
COQUETTE [*Seeing* PRUNELLA]. Oh!
CALLOW, MOUTH, DOLL. Oh!
ALL. Oh!
PRUNELLA [*Quietly*]. Oh, you are funny!
PIERROT. These are my friends. Now attention:
Callow!
CALLOW. Yes, I'm very young.
PIERROT. Doll!
DOLL. They say my heart's of sawdust.

28

PRUNELLA

PIERROT. Hawk!

HAWK. I pounce!

TAWDRY. Oh, not on me!

PIERROT. That's Tawdry—Mouth!

MOUTH. Greedy's my other name.

PIERROT. Romp!

ROMP. I'm the jolly girl.

PIERROT. Kennel, and Coquette!

KENNEL. I make no pretence to being nice.

COQUETTE. I'm here to waste his time.

PIERROT. Now, what's your name?

PRUNELLA. Of course I'm Prunella.

PIERROT. Well, I'm Pierrot.

ALL. Now you know.

PRUNELLA. Pierrot's a pretty name. [*She grows suddenly frightened.*] I think you'd better go away.

PIERROT. Oh, but that isn't polite of you.

PRUNELLA. I don't think my aunts would be pleased.

PIERROT. That shows their bad taste.

PRUNELLA. Oh, please go!—make haste!

PIERROT. No, we shan't.

PRUNELLA. Then I must. [*Begins to run.*

PIERROT. Catch my butterfly, catch my butterfly!
[*They circle round her.*

ALL. Butterfly! Butterfly!

HAWK. No, you're a chrysalis.

ROMP. Wait till the sun warms.

29

ACT 1   CALLOW. Then you shall fly away.

TAWDRY. Fly with us—not from us.

PRUNELLA. Oh, please stop—you make me so giddy.

PIERROT. Scaramel, bring her to me!

PRUNELLA. Go right away! Oh, what do you want?

PIERROT. What do I want?

SCARAMEL. Master, what do you want?

ALL. What do we want?

PIERROT. Well, I'm hungry.

PRUNELLA. Oh, are you? I'm sorry. I'll fetch you some bread in a minute.

ALL. Bread—dry bread? Oh, no.

PRUNELLA. And butter.

SCARAMEL. Bread and butter, miss!

PRUNELLA. Well, cake.

PIERROT. Neither bread, nor butter, nor cake.

PRUNELLA. Then you can't be really hungry.

PIERROT. Call it thirst. My lips are dry. Give me —give me a kiss.

ALL. Give him, oh give him a kiss.

DOLL. Do give him a kiss.

SCARAMEL. You're to give him a kiss.

PRUNELLA. That won't cure hunger and thirst.

PIERROT. It'll cure my hunger and thirst.

PRUNELLA. A kiss?

PIERROT. Just a kiss.

PRUNELLA. But that's nothing. I kiss people often —regularly.

ALL. Regularly—oh!

SCARAMEL. Never do things regularly.

PIERROT. To love—it's everything.

PRUNELLA. To love?

ALL. Love.

PRUNELLA. What is making you look so unhappy?

PIERROT. Love.

PRUNELLA. Is it love that has made you so pale?

PIERROT. Just love!

> [*The rest of the* Mummers *begin to adapt*
> *themselves to his mood and come, stepping*
> *solemnly, and listen. Sad music is heard.*

PRUNELLA. Alas! How sad a sight you are in truth!
Is love a thief, that you have lost your youth?
Why, you have turned quite white :
Your very clothes would seem to share your grief!

PIERROT. Yes, they went white when I did.

PRUNELLA. When was that?

PIERROT. Just now, when I first saw you from the
other side of the hedge.

PRUNELLA. You went white then?

PIERROT. As white as I could; I wasn't nearly so
white till I saw you.   At times I was so black I
ought to have been called Nero instead of Pierrot.
Ah! Now, don't be frightened—I wasn't *quite*
black, just a little bit off colour here and there, a
sort of magpie. You like magpies, don't you?—
women always do.

ACT I PRUNELLA [*Innocently*].   I never had a magpie.

PIERROT. Ah! I wish I had you in my nest! Oh-h!
> [*As he leans towards her*, PRUNELLA *instinctively draws back, and screens her face. Suddenly* PIERROT *falls into* SCARAMEL'S *arms.*

PRUNELLA. What's the matter?

COQUETTE. He's going to faint.

TAWDRY. He *has* fainted.

DOLL. I think he's going to die.

ROMP. He's dead.

PRUNELLA. No, he isn't.   Don't say such cruel things!

COQUETTE. Well, it will be your doing.

PRUNELLA. No, no!

DOLL [*Taking* PRUNELLA *by the arm, and pointing*].
Oh, poor Pierrot!   Look at him, look!

ALL [*Gather round, crying*].   O you poor, poor, poor Pierrot!
> [PIERROT *lies in* SCARAMEL'S *arms with eyes shut, and sighs.*

PIERROT [*Faintly*].   Yes, I hear what you are saying.   That's me, that's me.   Will nobody find me a remedy?

PRUNELLA. Oh, do, do, somebody find him a remedy!

COQUETTE. Somebody?

ALL. Find him a remedy somebody,
Somebody, somebody do!
From the way he's been taken,

Unless I'm mistaken,
That somebody ought to be you. [*To* PRUNELLA.

What is his malady?   Nobody,
Nobody, nobody knows;
Unless, by your pardon,   [*To* PRUNELLA.
You live in a garden,
With nothing that properly grows!

Find him a remedy somebody, etc.
      [*They seize* PRUNELLA, *and lead her up to him.*
PIERROT. Let her alone!   Let her go!
   Force is no remedy.
SCARAMEL.   No.
PIERROT. So the story will never come true?
PRUNELLA. What do you want me to do?
PIERROT. The man in the moon
   Came down too soon,
   And lost his heart to a maiden;
   With hunger and drouth,
   She burnt his mouth,
   And left him heavily laden.
DOLL.   ⎫
TAWDRY.   ⎬ Oh, cruel!
COQUETTE.   ⎭
PRUNELLA. Do you mean me?
PIERROT. Kiss me; then you will see.
PRUNELLA. But why do you wish for it so?
PIERROT. Kiss me—then you will know.
   c   33

ACT I ALL. Kiss him—then you will know.

> [*She kisses him. He meets the kiss passionately, holding her fast. She is overwhelmed, breaks from him, and runs into the house.*

PIERROT. And now—she knows.

> [*A pause.* COQUETTE *steals up to* PIERROT.

COQUETTE. Was it nice?

PIERROT. Get away!

ROMP. O Callow—wilt and die, and I'll kiss you to life!

HAWK. Oh, I'm lost to this earth. Rescue me, Tawdry, with your cherry lips!

PIERROT. Scaramel, turn them away!

SCARAMEL. Pack, baggages, pack!

KENNEL. On the road again—master of my master?

SCARAMEL. Yes. No, wait without.

DOLL. Well, since we've seen the show——

MOUTH. What a pretty piece of fooling!

SCARAMEL. Must I tell you twice?

TAWDRY. Save me, Hawk!

HAWK. By all means—my pigeon. [*Carries her off.*

THE OTHERS. Back we go—off we go, etc.

> [*They run off.*

SCARAMEL. Master! We are alone: we three.

PIERROT. We three?

SCARAMEL. You, and I, and the Key.

PIERROT. The Key?

SCARAMEL. It's the key of the garden gate.

PIERROT. What might it unlock for her!

SCARAMEL. Well, master—let's be getting on our way.

PIERROT. Once more.

SCARAMEL. I'll drop it here.

PIERROT. No, give it me!

SCARAMEL. Magic attends on us. This house has been blind and deaf. The magic's fading now.

PIERROT [*To himself*]. To-night, to-night!

SCARAMEL. Did you speak?

PIERROT. I am tempted—Scaramel.

SCARAMEL. Always yield to temptation.

PIERROT. Then to-night——

BOY [*Behind hedge*]. O you naughty, naughty birds, now will you?

Come into my garden, and I'll kill you!

    [PIERROT *pockets the key, and exit through hedge.*

O you naughty little pests, now fly, please!

Don't come making nests in *my* trees!

        [SCARAMEL *follows* PIERROT. *Curtain.*

ACT II

The same scene, night-time. The moon is rising away to the right of the stage. Its light crosses the top of the hedge, and strikes the head of the fountain-statue. The sound of keys and locking of gates is heard. Two gardeners enter with lanterns and keys. All lights are out in the house.

1st GAR. Ay, they are all a-bed.

2nd GAR. I'm about ready for mine.

1st GAR. [*Going off*]. It's going to be a clear night.

2nd GAR. Ay, full moon.   [*Exeunt.*

Enter PIERROT *and* SCARAMEL.

PIERROT. Scaramel.

SCARAMEL. Master.

PIERROT. Have you a ladder about you?

SCARAMEL. No, master.

PIERROT. That is very careless, to come out at night without a ladder.

SCARAMEL. Master, doubtless one can be procured.

PIERROT. One must be procured.

SCARAMEL. I hope, master, you are not doing this deliberately.

PIERROT. Give me my guitar.

SCARAMEL. *Your* guitar?

36

PIERROT. I bought it. Scaramel, I feel very happy ACT II
to-night.

SCARAMEL. Anticipation is always delightful.

PIERROT. And she shall be happy too.

SCARAMEL. She shall fulfil her little destiny.

PIERROT. I think she is different from any other.

SCARAMEL. You always think that, master.

PIERROT [*Offended*]. I am sure she is quite different
from every other.

SCARAMEL. O master, promise me you will be
selfish.

PIERROT. Scaramel, have you ever known me forget
myself?

SCARAMEL. Master, you are almost all I could wish.

PIERROT. Now for my serenade. Am I in voice
to-night?

SCARAMEL. The best that money could buy.

PIERROT. Tenor or baritone?

SCARAMEL. Both.

PIERROT. To-night I will sing tenor.

SCARAMEL. Three times for a tenor, twice for a
baritone.   [SCARAMEL *claps three times.*

Enter a TENOR.

PIERROT. Is this it?

SCARAMEL. This is it.

PIERROT. Can it speak as well?

SCARAMEL. I never inquired.

37

ACT II PIERROT [*To* TENOR]. Please remember, sir, that
I pride myself on my voice.

TENOR. Your voice?

PIERROT. Oh, you can speak?

TENOR. *Your* voice!

PIERROT. Well, I've paid for it. Now, Scaramel,
leave me to sing. [*Exit* SCARAMEL.

TENOR [*Sings*].

How now, everywhere up in air stars stare:
  On the roof shines the moon.
Little bird in your nest, are you there?
  Up, song, to her chamber go: say low, 'Down
    below,
  Thy love begs a boon.'
Little bird in your nest, are you there?

PIERROT. How strange my voice sounds to-night.

TENOR [*Sings*].

Sleep, sleep, for Love's sake let her wake,
  Say, 'Take no rest!'
Little bird in your nest, are you there?
  Tame heart, take heat, go beat in the small
    sweet breast.
Little dove, bird of Love, are you there?
Hour of night, at her bower go beat: say,
  'Sweet, now rise!'
Time flies! O Love, are you there?
Undo and renew to the night the light of your
  bright blue eyes!

38

PRUNELLA

For the man in the moon is here. ACT II
Do you hear? He is here!

PIERROT. Now stand back! [*He takes the* TENOR's
place.] Well? Well? Well??? Hasn't she
heard? Won't she answer? I sang that as finely
as ever I sang it. Come here, Tenor. Ah, I
understand. This means nothing to you—you
don't care a jot. You sing what you 're paid to
sing, not a note more. You professionals will be
the ruin of art. Don't answer me, sir. Off with
you! [*Exit* TENOR; *exit* PIERROT.

Enter SCARAMEL, *followed by* MOUTH *and* HAWK
bringing gardener's BOY *captive.*

SCARAMEL. Bring him along, bring him along!
BOY. Here, I say! You are pinching of me!
SCARAMEL. Are you pinching him, Hawk?
HAWK. No, but I will.
BOY. I 'll yell.
SCARAMEL. Don't let him yell.
MOUTH [*Putting his hand over* BOY's *mouth*]. Now
then. [HAWK *pinches him; an inarticulate sound.*
BOY. I did yell — inside myself; oh, and it
hurts!
SCARAMEL. That 's all right.
BOY. Ho, lor'! Why, you be the mummers. I
thought you was thieves.
SCARAMEL. Impudent bumpkin! Pinch him again!

39

ACT II BOY. Naow! Steady on, steady on. Why, I was
lookin' for you when you found me. Ha, ha!

ALL. Ba-a-a-a.

BOY. I want to run away with you and be a
mummer.

ALL. Oh!

CALLOW. That will be nice.

BOY. I'm glad you're glad. What's your name?

CALLOW. Christopherothchilyoctopusomegatommy-
rotempusemulsio Smith.

BOY. It's a nice little name. I'll get you to write
it down.

MOUTH. What shall we do with him?

SCARAMEL. What can you do, clodhopper?

KENNEL. Can you sing? Can you dance?

SCARAMEL. Can you find us a ladder?

BOY. What for?

SCARAMEL. Don't ask silly questions.

HAWK. Why, for fun.

BOY. There's one by the shed.

SCARAMEL. Fetch it.

BOY. To the right, round the corner.

SCARAMEL. Quietly.

[*Exeunt three of the* Mummers.

SCARAMEL. And so, my innocent young friend, you
want to see the world?

BOY. Ah, what I says is, give me Life.

SCARAMEL. Have you money?

40

Boy. No; I'll earn it by playing the fool.

Scaramel. Quite likely.

Boy. Just as you do.

Scaramel. Now you can't come alone.

Boy. Can't I?

Scaramel. Not with us; you must bring a maid with you.

Boy. Oh, I can wait on myself.

Scaramel. Come, is there no pretty maid in the house—one that you'd like to see Life with for a bit?

Boy. Oh, now I take you.

Scaramel. Whose window is that?

Boy. Oh, that's Aunt Prude's. I won't have *her*. She snores. Quiet now, and you'll hear her.

Scaramel. The next?

Boy. That's a passage.

Scaramel. Well, the one beyond?

Boy. Never you mind. I'll have her if she'll come. We must wait till to-morrow to ask.

Scaramel. That's Miss Prunella's?

Boy. You are quick.

Scaramel. Thank you, that's what I wanted to know.

Hawk. What now?

Scaramel. Oh, tie him up somewhere safe and quiet.

> [Scaramel *goes to fetch* Pierrot. *The ladder is brought on.*

41

ACT II Boy. Tie me up somewhere?

Hawk. No, nonsense! you're one of us now. Daredevil's your name.

Boy. No, it isn't.

Hawk. And now's your time to carry her off.

Boy. What! Wake her up at this time o' night?

Mouth. There's the ladder against her window.

Kennel. Now serenade her.

Boy. Sera——

Kennel. Sing to her.

Boy. My! That'd wake her.

Callow. Then up you go.

Mouth. And in at the window.

Boy. Oh, I'm feared she'd think I was intruding.

Hawk. Bah! you're afraid.

Boy. No, I ain't. But is it good manners? I've been brought up well.

Mouth. First you must sing. Here's my mandolin.

Boy. What must I sing?

Callow. That your heart is fluttering like a little dicky-bird.

Boy. I don't think I know that one.

Mouth. What do you know?

Boy. Well, will this do? 'O you naughty, naughty birds, now will you——'

[Pierrot *comes in, followed by* Scaramel.

Pierrot. What's this?

Boy. Now, you put me off.

Scaramel. Put him safe somewhere, didn't I tell you?

Hawk. Come now, you shall finish it later.

Boy. 'Come into my garden, and I'll'—what are you doing?

Kennel. Truss him tight.

Boy. This ain't part of the game.

Mouth. Yes, it is.

Boy. This ain't seeing Life.

Callow. Oh yes, it is.

Boy. Now you let me go, or I'll holler.

Hawk. Oh no, you won't.   [*Gags him.*

Scaramel. Now listen to me, my rustic friend. You're a clod, and must stay a clod. Don't be flying, or you'll come to grief. Can you hear me? That's right. Think it over till morning under the hedge. Now roll him away.

                [*They roll him up to the hedge.*

Hawk. Roly-poly gardener's boy.

Mouth. Safe like a hedgehog.

Callow. Good-night.

Mouth. Sleep well.

Scaramel [*To* Pierrot]. Yes, master, that's her window.

Pierrot. Ah, my bird,
          Be not too tame!

Scaramel. Master, we wait your word.

ACT II PIERROT. Come, comrades, then, stand back into the
 shade!
 Round us, night opens her sweet ears afraid,
 Dusk in her eyes.   Now call! and like a snare
 Send invitation up through the soft air,
 To that well-feathered nest that lacks its pair!

ALL [*Sing*].
 Sleeper, awake, arise, look out!

HAWK. The night owl calls and bats are about.

ALL. And we call too.   Come down, Pierrette!

ROMP. Here in our midst there's sport and to
 spare.

COQUETTE. Here with us there's a heart to share.

TAWDRY. Lie-a-bed, lie-a-bed, why d' you stay there.

ALL. What means waiting?   Come down, Pierrette!

KENNEL. Here over morals the moon throws a
 shade.

MOUTH. Here with us there's a game to be played.

HAWK. Here where the merry-thought waits for
 the maid.

ALL. Why are you waiting?   Come down, Pierrette!

CALLOW. Come and find comfort, come down, down,
 down!

DOLL. So we are to have another queen again?
 Will you serve her?

COQUETTE. Perhaps—as she deserves.

TAWDRY. I'll not.

ROMP. Ah, you're jealous.

 44

TAWDRY. I? What for! A mere penny-toy like ACT II
her?

PIERROT. The curtain stirred!

SCARAMEL. Back there into the shade!

> [*They all shrink back into the shade.* PIERROT *remains alone.* PRUNELLA *opens her window.*

PRUNELLA. Who is there? Who are you?

PIERROT. The man in the moon.

PRUNELLA. Oh! Why have you come back?

PIERROT. You called me! I came soon.

PRUNELLA. I?

PIERROT. You called me in a dream; and in a
dream I came.

PRUNELLA. No—for I have not slept.

PIERROT. You are asleep now. Will you not come
down?

PRUNELLA. Asleep?

PIERROT. Will you come down?

PRUNELLA. How can I come?

PIERROT. See! Out here waiting for you is a ladder
of dreams. Come down, and the dream will
come true!   [*Pauses. She makes no sign.*
Shall I come up and be your dream? Speak, give
me a sign!   [*She shakes her head.*
Then come down, and be mine!

PRUNELLA. Ah, but I dare not! Oh, what would
they say if they knew?

ACT II PIERROT. They would say nothing. They won't mind, they are asleep too.

People when sleeping come out of their shells and find wings:

Dreaming, they wake to a world full of beautiful things.

They become wise, they open their eyes and can see;

They become happy and young, they become free!

PRUNELLA. Pierrot, is it you, is it you that is saying all that; or is the world talking to me in its sleep?

PIERROT. It is the world, Pierrette, and Love!

PRUNELLA. Just now I heard voices calling me from below, and now I seem to hear them again.

PIERROT. Tell me what they say?

PRUNELLA. All the things I have ever said to myself and wished to be true. The trees say, 'Come and hide in us!' The grass says, 'Come and walk on me!' The dewdrops say, 'Come and dance with us!' And the air is like milk and honey to my lips as I lean out and breathe.

PIERROT. And the moon says, 'I am full of love, and my beams bring happiness!'

PRUNELLA [*Sighs*]. Ah!

PIERROT. Pierrette, it is already time for us to say good-bye.

46

PRUNELLA

PRUNELLA. Where are you going now?

PIERROT. To my playground, the world: where the gardens have no hedges and the roses no thorns, and where all birds fly free. Pierrette, Pierrette, come out of your cage! Come down!

PRUNELLA. I—I must! For a moment—for a moment only!

PIERROT. Life's but a moment.

> [PIERROT *makes a signal to* SCARAMEL, *who gives him* DOLL'S *cloak. He runs with it up the ladder and receives* PRUNELLA *in his arms.*

DOLL. Pff! I'm cold! It was I said I'd be nice to her, and now they take my cloak.

CALLOW [*Embracing her*]. Let me warm it again!

DOLL. I don't want you.

CALLOW. None of me? Oh, feel my heart!

ROMP. Oh, look, he's bringing her down!

ALL. Pierrette, Pierrette!

> [PIERROT *and* PRUNELLA *advance; he holds up his hand for silence. They all stop and become solemn.* PRUNELLA *stands very still.*

PIERROT. Now you are come, tell me what's in your mind.

PRUNELLA. The love I fear to lose, the love I find: Those who might miss me—those whom I might miss.

47

ACT II PIERROT. Forget, let the rest go! Remember this!
[*Kisses her on the lips.*

PRUNELLA. Ah!

PIERROT. Flower of night, flower of night!
Come and stand within the light,
And look into the heavens above,
Where the moon hangs like a hive,
And the stars are all alive;
For the stars are the bees of love.

Flower of night, flower of night!
My love and my delight!
Oh, come, and we will be there soon!
Where the night waits warm,
And the bees all in a swarm
Are hanging honey up to the moon!

Flower of light, dear delight,
Let our bed be there to-night!
Oh, come, and we will sleep there soon!
And there we will dwell,
Two hearts in one cell,
And eat up all the honey in the moon.

[*While the song goes on, the rest have crept
away, finger on lip, leaving the lovers alone.
Now they creep from behind the hedges, repeating the last line. A murmur of 'Queen-
bee, Queen-bee!' rises.*

PIERROT. Why do you stand so still?

48

PRUNELLA. It is too far
For me to go.
PIERROT. Why, what a child you are!
Do far things frighten you?
PRUNELLA. Where should I be
In the great empty world?
PIERROT. You 'd be with me.
PRUNELLA. Always?
PIERROT. Yes, practically always. Come!
PRUNELLA. No, loose my hands, let be! I must go
home.
PIERROT. Thy home is Love. Sweetheart, speak
truth and tell:
At this cold fountain learn Love's oracle!
> [*He leads her to the fountain: all the* Mummers
> *wrap themselves in cloaks and follow in
> procession; they stand looking on, while*
> PIERROT *and* PRUNELLA *advance towards
> the statue.*

PIERROT. Here turned to stone
The God of Flame
Stands all alone,
And mocks his name:
Bereft of breath
He stands and looks like death!

Mute on his viol
Lies his bow;

D 49

As on a dial
Here shadows show,—
O heavy crime!—
The waste, the waste of time!

PRUNELLA [*Kneeling*].
O stony youth,
Mute lips, blind eyes,
Reveal the truth!
Awake, arise!
Tell me, oh, tell,
If Love indeed be well!

[*Pause.* LOVE *wakes. He draws his bow
across his viol and speaks.*

LOVE. Yea, hearken to the lips of Love!
Where he abideth all is well,
His eyes do move the stars above,
He holds the Heavens beneath his
spell;
And in thy heart thou hear'st the chime
Of Love whose feet shall outrun time.

[*The* Mummers *make a circle about the lovers,
and move slowly round them in solemn pro-
cession.*

PRUNELLA. I hear the sound, I must obey!
Ah, where am I since yesterday?

PIERROT. Years, and a hundred leagues away!

PRUNELLA. There I find thee, O swiftest foot on
earth!

PIERROT. So runs my wish: [*To himself.*]—which ACT II
    yesterday had birth.
PRUNELLA [*Turning to look back at her window*].
  Yet see, look there : how desolate it seems !
  Let me go back and gather up my dreams,
  Where I have slept so well !
PIERROT.   You must forget
  Your former dreams, now you are Pierrette.
PRUNELLA. Why force me thus to go ?
PIERROT. Nay, you are free.
PRUNELLA. Let me stay here !
PIERROT. Then do not come with me.   [*Pause.*

    See yonder star, and yonder see !
    And, up above, the milky way !
    But yonder is the star for thee,
    Where we shall be ere dawn of day,—
    Up hill, down dale, and far away.
PRUNELLA. One hangs on yonder cypress spray :
    Nay, look how pale and wan for proof
    He hangs, imploring me to stay !
    And one goes down behind the roof.
    Where shall I be ere dawn of day ?
PIERROT. Years, and a hundred leagues away !
    [*A dance begins round the two lovers. At
       intervals* LOVE *strikes a note on his viol
       which gives the beat to the other music.
       The Columbines take off* PRUNELLA'S *cloak*

and reveal her as a PIERRETTE. *They pelt her with white blossoms, till she seems a cloud of flowers. At the end of the dance* PIERROT *advances and crowns her with a wreath of flowers.*

PIERROT. What you have dreamed to-night, do not forget.

Farewell, Prunella!

PRUNELLA.   I am—Pierrette!

[LOVE *strikes a note on his viol.* PRUNELLA *throws up her arms in a gesture of surrender, and flies into* PIERROT'S *arms. He lifts her bodily and carries her away. There is a burst of laughter from the* Mummers: *they pelt the statue with flowers, and romp off. After a minute enter the two gardeners with heavy staves and a lantern. The cuckoo clock in the house strikes three. They search round timorously and scratch their heads. One of them sees the open window and ladder, and mounts to look into the empty chamber. The gardener's* BOY *rolls out from under the hedge, frightening the other gardener terribly.* LOVE *draws his bow, and strikes a triumphant note. The gardener dashes towards him and strikes him with his staff. The bow falls broken from* LOVE'S *hand.*

52

ACT III

*Three years have elapsed. Sunset. The garden is overgrown, weedy,
and neglected. The fountain is moss-grown and thick with creepers.
The house-shutters are closed all but one or two; a notice 'To
Let' stands near.*

The BOY *is discovered dragging gardening tools across the stage in
a listless and desultory fashion, piling them on a bench, or packing
them into an open hand-barrow.*

BOY [*Sings dolefully*].
          My father said, my father said:
               What did my father say?
          'So long as you stands on yer 'ead
               You 're sure to find yer way!'
     'Ullo! there 's that bird again.   Waits till he sees
     me pack my clappers and then he begins of
     'imself.   Sh! Sh!   You just get out till I 'm
     gone!   Take that, and say I told yer!
          [*Throws stone, and then begins to wheel away
               hand-barrow.*
          Three years ago he told me so:
               But when my thoughts do run,
          Then all the work I 'ad to do
               I 'as to leave undone.

53

ACT III QUAINT [*Entering from house*]. Boy! here, boy!
Leave the spade.

BOY. Boy yerself! Who are you talking to?

QUAINT. Why don't you come when you are called?

BOY. If you requires to attrack my notice, you
better say 'Mister Gardener'; else I mayn't
'ear yer.

QUAINT. Pooh!

BOY. When you come into my garden, you acts
according. I don't come and poke my 'ead into
the 'ouse and say, 'Gal! old gal!' do I? Gardener's what I am now—same as I'm always
telling yer.

QUAINT. Fine gardener indeed!

BOY. '*Ead* gardener.

QUAINT. Well, I doubt if the new owner'll take *you*
on, when he sees the state the garden is in now.
Have you taken all the tools down to the
cottage?

BOY. If you'd eyes in yer 'ead you'd see. 'T's what
I'm doing now.

QUAINT. Mistress informed me to tell you that she
wants all the flowers from Miss Prunella's garden
taken. You'd better come back for them after-
wards: leave the spade!

BOY. Leave the garden! There's missis's bell a-
hollering for yer! You go, or you'll catch it.

QUAINT. Pho!

[*Exit into house.*

BOY [*Trails across to bench, leaves broom, and takes* ACT III *spade with him, crossing in front of statue*]. What are you looking at me for?—ain't said nothing to you. [*Retires up with hand-barrow. Enter* PRIVACY *followed by* QUAINT: *she descends slowly and enters the garden.* QUAINT *locks the door and signals contemptuously to* BOY *to go.* PRIVACY *sighs,* QUAINT *echoes her with exaggerated sentiment to convey sympathy and attract approval. Exit* BOY *slowly, imitating* QUAINT'S *sigh as he goes.*]

QUAINT. Hem!

PRIVACY. Have you the keys? Is everything locked now?

QUAINT. Everything that would lock, ma'am! Some of the keys won't work.

PRIVACY. Oh, it doesn't matter. There's nothing here that any one would want to take.

QUAINT. Are we to wait and give the keys to the gentleman?

PRIVACY. Yes, he will be here presently.

QUAINT. Well, I do wonder, if he's such a rich gentleman as they say he is, how ever he can care to come and live in such a place—as it is now.

PRIVACY. He does not intend to live here.

QUAINT. Oh, if he only means to die here, the place'll suit him well enough! [*Softening.*] I

ACT III beg your pardon, ma'am, I didn't mean anything.
It wasn't that I was thinking about—though
what's a black dress for, if it isn't to make you
hang your head like a tear-drop? No, ma'am, it's
only this lonesomeness gets so on one's nerves. I
wonder you could bring yourself to stay as long
as you have.

PRIVACY. I had recollections to keep me here.

QUAINT. Ah, my poor mistresses! They wouldn't
have wished to see you here, with the place like
this—all so shamefaced as it looks now!

PRIVACY. I had other reasons, Quaint.

QUAINT. I dare say you had, ma'am. Most people
have reasons for doing foolish things.

PRIVACY. I thought that some day Prunella might
come back, and I could not bear the thought of
her finding nobody here—or only strangers.

QUAINT. Oh, don't trouble yourself, ma'am! She
won't come back. She has forgotten you. She
doesn't care!—going off like that with a lot of
giddy-gaddies.

PRIVACY. Perhaps it was we who drove her away.

QUAINT. I don't think she took much driving.

PRIVACY. We old maids forget what youth is like.
Perhaps—without meaning to—we made life too
hard for her.

QUAINT. Ah, well, she has got the making of that in
her own hands now, and they're about full, I'll

56

be bound. Psh! You were always softer than ACT III
the others. I never heard them say a word. I'd
like to have seen her daring to put her nose in
here while they were alive!

PRIVACY. Hush! [*A bell rings.* PRIVACY *looks
agitated.*]

QUAINT. Good lud! ma'am, why do you start like
that? Now you're all of a tremble.

PRIVACY. I always think and hope——

QUAINT. The gate always stands open, ma'am.
She'd never ring the bell.

PRIVACY. No, she'd never ring the bell. The gate
stands open always, and at night a lamp has burnt.

QUAINT. Shall I go, ma'am?

PRIVACY. Of course. This must be he.

[QUAINT *goes.*

How poor the place is; weeds are everywhere.
Dead leaves beneath one's feet, rustling like
  memories:
Poor, restless ghosts of unforgotten time.

Enter PIERROT *and* SCARAMEL, *shown in by* QUAINT.

PRIVACY. Sir, you are very punctual.

PIERROT. Am I punctual, Scaramel?

SCARAMEL. Master, we have accomplished twenty-
one miles in fifty-five minutes.

PIERROT. That seems slow. So this is the place I
remember.

PRIVACY. You have been here before?

PIERROT. Once upon a time. A charming dull spot. But changed, but changed.

PRIVACY. You don't find what you expected?

PIERROT. Scaramel, did I expect anything?

SCARAMEL. My master now makes it his rule never to expect anything. So he is never disappointed.

PIERROT. You wonder, madam, what my interest in buying such a place can be. I once picked up here, by chance, a treasure, a trinket, which I have since lost.

PRIVACY [*With sudden intuition*]. Prunella?

PIERROT. I beg your pardon.

PRIVACY. Prunella, Prunella, Prunella!

PIERROT. I had forgotten her name.

SCARAMEL. We called her by some other.

PRIVACY. It was you, it was you!

PIERROT. Yes, it was I.

PRIVACY. Where is she now?

PIERROT. I often wonder.

PRIVACY. Oh, we forgave her going; almost we would have forgiven you the theft. But you are heartless.

PIERROT. That is true. How did you find it out? No matter. Every one finds me out now.

PRIVACY. But tell me all you know.

PIERROT. Tell her, Scaramel.

SCARAMEL. Madam, the story is not interesting ACT III
unless my telling make it so; and there is much
that you may not understand. I think we may
claim that we educated her. Her education,
madam, was very deficient; she had been much
neglected. Life was a dead letter to her. We
taught her everything. She learned to dance, to
laugh, to sing, to love. For a time it seemed
that there was nothing she could not learn. She
loved my master very faithfully, and my master
accepted the situation like a man. He has a tender
heart, he likes to see happy faces around him, and
so he took a step which—not through his own
fault—led to a little misunderstanding.

PIERROT. Scaramel, I am disposed to tell this myself. But stay near me: I may need prompting.
What was that original remark I made about
women the other day, Scaramel?

SCARAMEL. Master, you said they puzzled you.

PIERROT. Ah! It is still true. They are so illogical.
Think, madam, she said she loved me and yet she
left me! Well, you shall hear. For two years—
it was two years, was it not, Scaramel?—for two
happy years we had wandered together from place
to place, seeing the world—foreign countries, and
people, and gay towns. We danced, we laughed,
we sang. We were married—she had wished it.
[*He shrugs.*] People laughed when I told them

that. 'Pierrot married!' they said, 'Oh no!—unless he has married a dozen.' But we were married—that was what made things difficult. I wasn't used to being married—it's outside my habits altogether: it was strange, and everybody laughed so. And one day it seemed so foolish that I—went away and left her.

PRIVACY. You said that she left you.

PIERROT. Ah, not then, not then! That was later. I left her—saying nothing: it is so much easier to say nothing when you've nothing to say. But before I went I had given her a lot of money, and a lot of pretty things, dresses, trinkets, bon-bons —everything I could think of to make her happy —except—my love. [*He begins to be carried away by his story, and to lose his pose of indifference.*] I took that with me. And presently I found I couldn't get rid of it; and it grew heavier and heavier, till my heart began to—what did my heart begin to do, Scaramel?

SCARAMEL. Your heart became bad company, Master.

PIERROT. Yes, it was quite distressing! I couldn't amuse myself: I couldn't dance, or laugh, or sing. It always came and caught me by the throat, and said, or seemed to say, ' You thief! you fool!' I tried cures; but they were no good. And so, and so—at last I went back to see if the cure was there.

PRIVACY. Yes?

PIERROT. I had been gone a whole year; but I came back again. You see, now—it was not I who left her; she didn't wait for me long enough. There was the little house, just as I had left it: she hadn't taken a penny, she hadn't touched a thing. Even the last thing I gave her before I went I found lying covered over with dust inside the empty house which I opened with my own key. And in the garden was a small stone, and on it was written: 'Here lies— Pierrette.'

PRIVACY. Who was 'Pierrette?'

PIERROT. You may explain that, Scaramel.

SCARAMEL. Pierrette was the name of my master's love for her. She probably goes by some other name now, if she is still alive. To us, of course, she chose to die. What may have happened since——

PRIVACY. You neither know nor care.

SCARAMEL. It was an episode.

PRIVACY. I thank you for the story, sir.

SCARAMEL. Not at all. My master rather likes to relate it. I notice it grows late. We expect guests. They are almost due.

PRIVACY. I will leave you in full possession. My maid will hand you the keys.

[QUAINT *talks to* SCARAMEL.

ACT III PIERROT. Madam, this seems almost like turning you out.

PRIVACY. My means no longer permit me to live where I would wish.

PIERROT. That is a pity!—not to be able to do as one wishes. And you have grown to be a part of the place: its atmosphere clings round you. Do you mean to go—quite away?

PRIVACY. To a cottage beyond the gates. I dare not go as far as I would wish. She might return.

PIERROT. She—might—return. Scaramel! Have you any——? [SCARAMEL *gives him his purse.*] I fear you are poor?

PRIVACY. My poverty is not of your making, and my sorrow money will not buy from me. I will intrude no longer.   [*Exit* PRIVACY.

PIERROT. Really, Scaramel, have you no repartee?

SCARAMEL. Master, I was not listening.

PIERROT. Then that was as well. Give me the key of the house.

SCARAMEL [*To* QUAINT]. Give me the key of the house.

QUAINT. There are the keys.

SCARAMEL. Which is it?

PIERROT. Quickly, quickly.

SCARAMEL. Is it a large key?

QUAINT. No, it's a small key. [*He finds a key.*] ACT III
  That is the key of the garden gate.

PIERROT and SCARAMEL [*Guiltily startled*]. Eh?

QUAINT. That's the house key. [PIERROT *takes it.*]

PIERROT. It's not a watch-key, nor a bed-key, not
  a watch-key, nor a bed-key. [*Goes into house.*]

SCARAMEL. Dear me, now!

QUAINT. Your master's mad, I don't mind telling
  you.

SCARAMEL. Original, my good woman: at the most,
  eccentric. It suits him.

QUAINT. And he's a villain.

SCARAMEL. My good woman, if you were a little
  more up in the world——

QUAINT. And if you were a little more up in the
  world—upon a ten-foot gallows, you and your
  master too—the world 'd be sweeter. He's a
  rogue.

SCARAMEL. If you were more up in the *ways* of the
  world, you 'd know that it's usual for us to abuse
  our own masters, not each other's.

QUAINT. Well, my mistress is a fool, but he's a
  scoundrel. What's he come back here for?

SCARAMEL. Would you understand if I said 'to lay
  a ghost'?

QUAINT. No, I shouldn't.

SCARAMEL. Then I won't tell you.

QUAINT. Ghost indeed! He's little better himself!

ACT III   A whited sepulchre's what he is. Silkworms 'll eat him! I can see his angling skeleton grinning out of him already. Yours too. Yours is a black one. Whalebone.

SCARAMEL. My good woman, you have no dignity. Masters aren't worth quarrelling about. They mean wages, nothing more. There are good places and bad places. Now, I'm busy: you'd better go!

QUAINT. Well, you'll find your place some day. [*Points down.*]   [*Exit* QUAINT.

SCARAMEL [*Smiling*]. Now that's a woman's way of saying it, and neat too. Well, I must buck; there's a lot to be done!

Enter KENNEL.

CALLOW [*Outside*]. O you little moulting birds, now will you?
Come into my garden, and I'll kill you!

Enter CALLOW.

KENNEL. What ho, Scaramel! Hark to this belated youth!

SCARAMEL. That's just what he is, a belated youth. Where are the rest?

KENNEL. How should I know? Lost their way, most likely.

64

SCARAMEL. Well, you 've found yours. You are in ACT III luck.

Re-enter BOY, *with spade on shoulder.*

BOY. Why, it 's the mummers!

CALLOW. Who 's that? What has he got in his hand?

KENNEL. A spade!

CALLOW. Who are you?

BOY. Me? 'Im as you tied up and put under the 'edge that night. Saucy 'ounds you was, too!

SCARAMEL. And what are you here for now?

BOY. 'Ere for now? Why, I 'll tell yer—what I 'as to tell everybody—I 'm 'ead gardener here now; and I 'm diggin' 'oles to bury you in—'ead downwards—make yer 'air grow, same as mine—so you won't know yerselves. [*Departing with dignity.*

CALLOW and KENNEL [*Laughing foolishly*]. Hee-hee! Hee-hee! Won't know ourselves, eh?
[*They stop abruptly.*

BOY [*Returning*]. Say, I 'm glad I didn't come with you when you ast me. Why, you are only a lot of scarecrows after all! Good-night, bawly 'eads; sleep well, and don't let the ghosts wake yer before it 's time. [*Exit.*

CALLOW. Ghosts? I don't like that fellow.

KENNEL. No; and he doesn't like us.

CALLOW. Once he wanted to come with us.

E

ACT III KENNEL. Times have changed.   Come, scarecrow!

CALLOW. What, you little jays and jackdaws, will you

Come into my garden, and I'll kill you!

[PIERROT *comes out of the house, and passes without observing them; they enter it.*

SCARAMEL. Have you any further orders, master?

PIERROT [*Abstractedly*].   Oh, go to Scaramel, ask him!   [SCARAMEL *starts.*

[PIERROT *goes towards fountain.*

Scaramel, who was that spoke to me just then?

SCARAMEL. Master, the air of this place is not good for you.   Would it not be better if——

PIERROT. If you changed it?   Yes, change it, Scaramel, change it by all means, if you can. Clear it of its vapours, tell the sun to rise, and the birds to sing!

Enter HAWK *and* MOUTH *with* TAWDRY.

TAWDRY. Lud, it's a weary way here.

MOUTH. I don't think much of the place, now we've got there.

HAWK. Why, then it's as well I can't see it.

SCARAMEL. Come, you'll feel better by supper-time.

MOUTH. No, my appetite's gone.

SCARAMEL. But you're still greedy.

MOUTH. I'm losing my teeth.

TAWDRY. Times have changed.

66

HAWK. Times have changed.

MOUTH. Times have changed.

> [*They go into the house.*

SCARAMEL. Master!

PIERROT. Alone at the end of the day,

As the sick world grins by,

Stands this house——

SCARAMEL. Master!

PIERROT. Eh?

SCARAMEL. The company arrives.

PIERROT. My friends?

SCARAMEL. Your guests.

PIERROT. Not the same thing, is it, Scaramel?

SCARAMEL. You will remember, sir, we are out of friends for the moment.   [DOLL *runs on.*

DOLL. Oh, I'm lost, I'm lost in this ugly garden. They've left me all alone.

PIERROT. Are you afraid?

DOLL. Yes, very.

PIERROT. What sort of company d'you want?

DOLL. I'm not particular.

PIERROT. No, truly. There's the house, get inside.

DOLL. Won't you come?

PIERROT. Not yet.   [DOLL *goes in.*

PIERROT. Who's that old woman?

SCARAMEL. Master, that's Doll with the painted smile and her little turned-in toes. You remember her?

PIERROT. She has grown old.

ACT III SCARAMEL. Then there's Hawk, and Callow, and Kennel, and Mouth.

PIERROT. Faithful followers of my purse.

SCARAMEL. Master, they must live.

PIERROT. They call it living.

SCARAMEL. Then there's Coquette.

PIERROT. Ah, she's been precious in her time.

SCARAMEL. H'm! her modesty's down at ankle now, like a slipt garter. Romp's a little heavier on the bounce than she used to be. Tawdry's much as usual, but dressed worse than ever, and costing more. The old faces, master, as you desired?

PIERROT. Well, if they'll help me to remember, or to forget. Either way, either way.

SCARAMEL. H'm! [*He goes into the house; laughter is heard.*

PIERROT [*Sits listless by fountain, and gazes all round and up at house*]. How now—

                        [*Fingers his guitar doubtfully.*
How now, everywhere, up in the air, stars stare!
Little bird in your nest, are you there?

                        [*Lets his guitar fall dejectedly.*
No answer!

                 [*After a pause he takes up his guitar again.*
Sleep, sleep, for God's sake let her wake! say, 'Take no rest'——!

                              [*He breaks off*

I forget, I forget the words that once came of ACT III
themselves.

Re-enter SCARAMEL, *with his fiddle.*

[*Angrily.*] Scaramel, there's no tune in these
strings. They are rusty.

SCARAMEL. Master, everything's rusty here, it seems
to me. Nothing goes right, everything wants oiling.
I shall have more on my hands than I can do.

PIERROT. Get the others to help you.

SCARAMEL. They are no good. One can't rouse
them. I think they want a new master.

PIERROT. Oh yes, find them one by all means.
What's the matter?

SCARAMEL. Kennel's guttering to his end. Callow's
brain is softening—what's left of it. Mouth has
become a jibberer; you can hear him now!
Hawk's as blind as a bat. Not one of them's
what he used to be. We are growing old, master.

PIERROT. Do you remember, Scaramel, that night?

SCARAMEL. Master, I remember many nights. At
what hour shall dancing begin?

PIERROT. Ah, how tender she was! How fresh and
young!

SCARAMEL. Master, at what hour?

PIERROT. Oh, when you like, when you like! She
stood by me here at this fountain. Do you
remember, Scaramel?

69

ACT III SCARAMEL. I will remember anything you wish,
master, as soon as we have made all the arrange-
ments.

PIERROT. Scaramel, I believe this stone remembers
more than you. You are very selfish, Scaramel.
Life to you is a meal; and there you sit at it,
with a napkin tucked up from your waist to your
chin, and you shut your eyes and open your
mouth and eat. And when you get up from it,
all your mind will be like a bill of fare; just a list
of the things you have eaten.

SCARAMEL. Possibly, master. The wines to-night
are——

PIERROT. Ah! [*Turns away in disgust, and strikes
his hand on the fountain.*

O Love, your fountain has run dry,
And have you lost your tongue?
Speak, stone!——
You see, Scaramel, he won't answer me now.

SCARAMEL. Love never does answer, master, if you
treat it too seriously.

PIERROT. That night this stone thing seemed to
have life and speech! The water sang to us, and
music seemed to come, one knew not whence.
Scaramel, have you noticed the statue's bow is
broken? I wish it repaired. See to it.

SCARAMEL. Instantly, master!
[*He lays his fiddle-bow in its hand.*

70

PIERROT. Here turned to stone　　　　　　　　
　　　The God of Flame
　　　Stands all alone,
　　　And mocks his name.
　　　Bereft of breath
　　　He stands and looks like death.

　　　　　　　　　　　　　[*A pause.*

　That was not the music of it.
SCARAMEL. Master, there will be musicians.
PIERROT. But they're mechanical.　Hark to that
　bird, the last in this garden, I think.
　Sweet, sweet, sweet, throw it a crumb.
SCARAMEL. Five courses for supper.　Three wines.
　And the dancing.
　　　　　　　　[*He begins to count on his fingers.*
PIERROT. Ah, there again.　Sweet, sweet, sweet!
　No, Bitter sweet, bitter sweet, bitter, bitter,
　bitter!　Yes, that fits best.　So you've learned
　the word too, have you, little bird?　Have you
　been round the world and loved more than you
　meant to, and come back again, and found your-
　self all alone?　And forgetting—forgetting—No.
Scaramel!　Scaramel!　　　　　　[*As he remembers.*

　　Alone, at the end of the day
　　　While the gay world ran by,
　　Stood a house with a heart of decay,
　　　Almost ready to die.

　　　　　　　　　　　　　　　　71

ACT III And everything there seemed to wait;
   For the hedges were thin;
And a notice was up at the gate,
   Begging Love to come in.

But Love cannot read—he is blind,
   So he came there one day;
And deeming the owner unkind,
   He went his own way.

No, no!   For the doors were set wide,
   And the windows unfast,
And at night, while the householder sighed,
   Love entered at last.
                                       [*A gong is heard.*

PIERROT [*Panic-stricken*].   What's that?

SCARAMEL. Supper is served.

PIERROT [*Recovering himself*].   That matters most.
          [PIERROT *goes in, followed by* SCARAMEL.
             Daylight passes into dark.   Intermezzo.

Enter PRUNELLA. *She sinks down, utterly worn out.*
          Re-enter SCARAMEL.

SCARAMEL. What are you doing here, beggar-girl?

PRUNELLA. I've come home.

SCARAMEL. Some mistake, I think.

PRUNELLA. Scaramel!

SCARAMEL. That's my name, and no property of
   yours.

PRUNELLA. Don't you remember me?

SCARAMEL. No.

Enter DOLL *and* COQUETTE.

DOLL. Scaramel! Scaramel!
COQUETTE. Don't stay away.
DOLL. He's so strange to-night.
COQUETTE. You understand him.

[*Exit* SCARAMEL.

PRUNELLA. Coquette! Doll!
COQUETTE and DOLL. Who's this?
PRUNELLA. Don't you remember me?
COQUETTE and DOLL. No.
PRUNELLA. I was Prunella, I am Pierrette.
COQUETTE and DOLL. Say it again.
PRUNELLA. Oh!

Enter TAWDRY *and* ROMP.

TAWDRY. Doll and Coquette!
ROMP. You're to come back.
COQUETTE. No. Come and look here.
DOLL and COQUETTE. She was Prunella, she is
    Pierrette. We don't remember her, do we?
TAWDRY and DOLL. No.
PRUNELLA. You loved me once, you said you loved
    me.
TAWDRY and ROMP. Did we?
COQUETTE. When was that?
ROMP. Was it yesterday?
DOLL. Or the day before?

ACT III COQUETTE. I only just remember yesterday.

TAWDRY. I can't remember the day before; I never could.

DOLL. Nor I.

ROMP. And as for last week——

COQUETTE. Or last month, or last year.

DOLL. Why, I always forget how old I am.

COQUETTE and DOLL. We 're very sorry.

ROMP and TAWDRY. But it can't be helped, can it?

PRUNELLA. But what are you doing here? This is my home.

DOLL and COQUETTE. Is it?

TAWDRY and ROMP. We don't know.

PRUNELLA. This was my home.

COQUETTE. Perhaps it has forgotten you too.

DOLL. You 're very ragged.

PRUNELLA. I am poor.

TAWDRY. And pale.

PRUNELLA. I 'm weary.

ROMP. And downcast.

PRUNELLA. I 'm disappointed.

ALL FOUR. No wonder that we can't remember you.

PRUNELLA. I have come so far, and now, no welcome.

ROMP. Are you hungry too?

PRUNELLA. I dare say.

ROMP. Well, if I were you I 'd get some food from somewhere. You 'll feel better then!

[SCARAMEL *comes back*.

SCARAMEL. Now, baggages, you're called for.

PRUNELLA. Scaramel, where's your master?

SCARAMEL. In the house.

PRUNELLA. I must see him.

SCARAMEL. Oh, indeed, no! He wouldn't remember
you. Besides, he never lets me remind him of
unpleasant things while he is at supper.

PRUNELLA. Then where is my home?

COQUETTE. She's come a long way.

ROMP. She's poor.

TAWDRY. She's very tired.

DOLL. And disappointed.

PRUNELLA. Where are those I once lived with—
those who loved me?

SCARAMEL. Dead, I dare say.

PRUNELLA. Dead?

COQUETTE. Now she'll cry.

DOLL. Oh, how unpleasant.

TAWDRY. I can't bear seeing people cry.

ROMP. If she means to cry, she must be sent away.

SCARAMEL. Baggages, get in!

DOLL. I do detest these scenes.

TAWDRY. So inconsiderate.

COQUETTE. People should keep their self-respect.

ROMP. I gave her very good advice. But then I'm
worldly wise.   [*They go into the house.*

SCARAMEL. Now, you'd better be getting along,
beggar-girl.

ACT III PRUNELLA. Where?

SCARAMEL. That's your business, isn't it? Far be it from me to interfere.

PRUNELLA. I'm weary.

SCARAMEL. You can sit down outside.

PRUNELLA. I'm weary of life.

SCARAMEL. Ah, that's what all you useless people say.

PRUNELLA. Useless?

SCARAMEL. My girl, no doubt you've been pretty in your time. . . . Well, good looks as a livelihood don't last. . . . Stir about, find some other occupation. . . . It's useless maundering there about what's gone!

PRUNELLA. Does nothing last?

SCARAMEL. Nothing I know of.

PRUNELLA. Does love never last?

SCARAMEL. Now don't you know it doesn't?

PRUNELLA. Yes, I know. No, I deny that; for my love has lived,—will live for ever though I die!

SCARAMEL. Yes, but what's the use?

PRUNELLA.—As I pray to die.

SCARAMEL. Ah, dying isn't so easy either.

PRUNELLA. In the spring my life began;
In the summer—happiness!
In the autumn let me die.

SCARAMEL. Yes, it's a depressing time of year, and

such an untidy one. Consider this garden. Look ACT III
here, young woman, here's a way for you to be
useful. If you want to earn twopence—well, say
threepence—find a broom and sweep up here.
It's more than the market value of the work, but
no matter. Only be gone by the time we've
finished supper, for really you're not fit to be
seen. D'ye hear? Oh well, gratitude is out of
fashion. If you want the money, go round for it
to the back door.   [SCARAMEL *goes.*

PRUNELLA [*Stands dazed for a while and then
speaks*]. No one remembers me. [*She looks
round for a broom; finding it, she begins to sweep
up the leaves. Then her eyes fall on the fountain.
To the Statue.*]
Oh yes! you—you—you must remember me,
For it was you! It was you!
Why did you speak?
Had you no pity for a heart so weak
As mine? Nay, Love, what made you do this
     wrong?
You spoke, and all the world became a song,
And all my heart a bird that heard its mate
Calling and crying to it disconsolate,
Bidding me come!
Say you remember me!
          [*A burst of laughter, clapping of hands, and
            cries of 'Bravo' are heard from the house.*

ACT III

She turns to the Statue in a frenzy, and falls, beating her hands against the stone.

O stony youth!
Dumb lips, blind eyes,
Tell me the truth,
Awake, arise!
Say, where does folly dwell, if Love be wise?
        [*She falls half senseless at his feet.* LOVE *draws his bow over his viol, and speaks.*

LOVE. Nay, hearken to the lips of Love!
Where Love endureth, all is well.
He lighteneth the stars above,
He holds the heavens beneath his spell.
Even in thy grief abides the sound
Of Love that girds the whole world round.

PRUNELLA. Dark is that world henceforth about
    me!

LOVE.   Yet,
Couldst thou so will it, yet would thy heart forget
Its love?   [*A pause: she sobs.*
Nay, nay,—so long hast thou been wise—
Forsake not wisdom now!

PRUNELLA.   Oh that mine eyes
Could fail as daylight fails, and all my breath
Melt into air and leave me alone with death!
Hast thou no well of waters here, where I
May drown my sorrow?

LOVE. Nay, my bed is dry   ACT III
For lack of true love's tears.

PRUNELLA. Here at thy brink
My long-stored griefs shall give thee tears to
drink!

LOVE. And having wept thy fill, what gift might
best
Afford thee comfort?

PRUNELLA. I would be at rest
Where under earth or sea it lies most deep!

LOVE. Here lay thee down! Cover thyself and
sleep!
I'll be thy watcher. Here shalt thou forget,
Past griefs and present. Good-night, Pierrette!
        [*Pause: she goes to the fountain.*

PRUNELLA. Good-night, Love, and good-night,
sorrow!
     [*She lies down and covers herself with leaves.*

LOVE. Good-night, Pierrette! Pierrette, good-
morrow!
     [*Sleep music. The light fades from* LOVE'S
     face. Mummers *rush on, laughing.*

SEVERAL. { Here we come,
{ Look at us;
{ Rowdy and rackety!

KENNEL. Life's none so bad after supper.

CALLOW. Wine, wine is my only love.

DOLL. And me, and me, and me.

ACT III CALLOW. You're a good second.

HAWK. I can see now; oh! most extraordinary things.

MOUTH. Here we come!

TAWDRY. Look at us!

ROMP. Rowdy and rackety!

SCARAMEL. That's right. Be merry! Sing louder! Sing louder! You're paid for it, aren't you?

KENNEL. As my joints unstiffen so I kick, kick, kick.

MOUTH. Jump little Tawdry, jump so high.

DOLL. What a wretched old garden!

HAWK. Who pulled it to pieces? [PIERROT *enters.*

PIERROT. Ah, right, right, right! This is youth, this is youth!

SCARAMEL. Is this as you wish it?

PIERROT. Is this as it was?

SCARAMEL. Almost.

PIERROT. Ah, true. She is not here.

SCARAMEL. Won't one of these do?

PIERROT. Which?

SCARAMEL. Doll? Coquette?

PIERROT. If she were dead, would not her ghost haunt this garden?

SCARAMEL. Master!

DOLL. Oh, how unpleasant!

COQUETTE. Don't frighten us.

DOLL. Things were becoming so pleasant again.

PIERROT'S SERENADE

(FROM 'PRUNELLA')

Laurence Housman.   Joseph Moorat.

How now, ev-ery-where up in   air   stars stare: On the   roof   shines the

moon.   Lit-tle bird in your   nest, are you there, are you   there?

rit.   *mf accel.*   *p*   *cres. accel.*

there?   Tame heart, take heat,   go   beat   in the small sweet   breast.   Lit-tle

rit.   *a tempo.*   *p*   *cres. accel.*

cres. accel.   *animato.*   *ritar.*

dove,   bird   of Love,   are   you there,   are   you   there?

cres.   *accel.*   *ritar.*   *a tempo.*   *p*

appassionato.

p   *cres.*   *mf.*   *dim.*   *p*

Hour   of night,   at   her   bow - er   go beat: say, 'Sweet, now a - rise,'   Time   flies!   O

dim.   *p*

Love,   are   you   there,   are   you   there?   Un - do   and   re-

new to the night the light of your bright blue eyes! For the man in the moon is here.

Do you hear? He is here! Do you hear? He is here!

PIERROT. I wonder, could we raise it?

SCARAMEL. Master, be warned!

MOUTH. Here we are!

TAWDRY. Look at us!

CALLOW. Rowdy and——

PIERROT. Sh! With due preparation. That was her window. See, I remember.

ROMP. Oh, don't you do it!

HAWK. What's all this? I'm going blind again.

MOUTH. No, the night has fallen.

PIERROT. A ladder against the window just as once upon a time.

SCARAMEL. Master, we don't believe in ghosts.

PIERROT. Scaramel, I'm getting tired of your beliefs. Do as you're told. Also there must be moonlight.

SCARAMEL. There's no moon to-night.

PIERROT. Are you sure? Put out the torches.

DOLL. Oh, not the dark, please!

COQUETTE. We're very much afraid.

PIERROT. No moon? are you sure? Memory and magic surround us. [*The torches are put out.*] We awake. [*Moonlight.*] It seems long since I saw the moon. Now quietly, quietly about your business—go.

[*The* Mummers *go off.*

SCARAMEL. Master, let me tell you, this is very foolish.

F

ACT III PIERROT. How good to be foolish again!

    [SCARAMEL *goes after the others.* PIERROT *is
    left alone and despondent.*

LOVE. O you naughty, naughty bird, now will you?
Come into my garden, and I'll kill you!

PIERROT [*Turns about, startled*].

    Who called? I thought that I heard some one
    cry

    'Pierrot! Pierrot, come out and die!'

Is no one here at all?   [*He goes towards house.*

LOVE.   No one.

PIERROT.   Who's there?

    What is this echo answering me in air?

    [*He turns.* LOVE *nods to him.* PIERROT
    shrinks back, shivering with fear.

LOVE. So you have come back?

PIERROT [*Recovering his courage*]. So you are
awake again?

LOVE. It wasn't you who woke me!

PIERROT. Now, where is she? Say!

LOVE. What, have you lost her?

PIERROT. Well, I let her go.

LOVE. Wasn't that careless?

PIERROT. Careless, no!

LOVE. Cruel, then?

PIERROT. Yes, to myself.

LOVE. Oh, self, self, self, still self!

PIERROT. That is my burden; take it from me!

LOVE. Do you forget that I am stone? Call ACT III
her.

PIERROT. I have called—secretly.

LOVE. Not from your heart, only for vanity.

PIERROT. All, all is vanity!

LOVE. So you have found that out. Well, you 're
still tolerably young. There 's hope in youth.
Good-night, Pierrot.

PIERROT. Where is she? Answer me, speak, speak,
I say!

LOVE. How can I, when I 'm stone, you fool?

PIERROT. You fool! *[He sinks down in despair.*
[The Mummers *return with the ladder.*

HAWK. Quietly, quietly,
Here comes the ladder.

KENNEL. Rickety, rackety,
Mildewed and cobweby,
Half the rungs broken.

MOUTH. Bats bodies hung on it,
Owls made a roost of it,
Rats' teeth have gnawed it:
There in a corner we found it forgotten.

CALLOW. Quietly, quietly,

HAWK. Up to the window there,
Rear it and leave it.

ROMP. Who means to venture there?

COQUETTE. Who will go up on it?

TAWDRY. Who will come down on it?

ACT III DOLL. Nobody—nobody.

PIERROT. Nobody—nobody.

HAWK. Who is to tap at the window now?

CALLOW. I won't knock at an empty house.

ROMP. Ghosts might hear us and hang out their
heads.

MOUTH. In long white night-caps wagging their
skulls.

DOLL. Oh, don't! You frighten me!

PIERROT. Hush!

KENNEL. Yes, I hear something.

PIERROT. See!

HAWK, MOUTH, DOLL, ROMP. See, it opens.

COQUETTE. Yes.

MOUTH. No one is there!

KENNEL. But the window is opening.

SCARAMEL. Master, master, it is only the wind.

PIERROT. Well, it's an ill wind that blows no man
good.

SCARAMEL. That old ladder won't bear you!

PIERROT. Let it break!

SCARAMEL. Master! are you insured?

PIERROT. Go! to the Devil who sent you! Take
your wage!

[*Exit* SCARAMEL.

ALL. Sleeper, undo your door, look out!
The night wind blows, there are ghosts about,—
Ghosts underground and ghosts in air!

84

PRUNELLA

PIERROT. Little bird, in your nest, are you there?

ALL. Under the leaves small skeletons hang,—
　Skeleton leaves where the birds once sang.
　Come down now, and be one of the gang!

PIERROT. Love, Love, are you there? are you
　there?

ALL. Ferret her out, however decayed,
　Old and decrepit: here once lived a maid:—
　Honey her heart was.

PIERROT. Love, are you there?

ALL. Walls are to climb and windows to break.
　Sleep all day, but at night lie awake,
　Lest under the shadow thieves enter and take!

PIERROT. Sleep, sleep, for God's sake let her
　wake!
　　　　Love, Love, are you there?

　　　　　　　　　　　　　[*Rushes up ladder.*
　　　　No one is there, I am alone.
　　　　Pierrette! Pierrette! Pierrette!

COQUETTE. Come away!

TAWDRY. I daren't look.

DOLL. He frightens me.

　　　　　　　　[PRUNELLA *rises from the fountain.*

ROMP. Oh, look, look, look!

DOLL. Oh, let's get away!

COQUETTE. It is her ghost!

TAWDRY. Look, she is coming up out of the ground.
　Oh!

85

ACT III   SEVERAL. { Oh yes, it is she!   It is she!
Don't stay here any longer!
Let's run, let's run!

[*Exeunt all except* PIERROT *and* PRUNELLA.

PRUNELLA. Pierrot, come down!   Pierrot, lift up
   your head,
   Come from your cage, come down!   Pierrot,
      they said
   That you did not remember me at all!
   And yet out of my sleep I heard you call
   My name!
   And when you called—I came.

[*He descends, and stands gazing at her motionless.*

PIERROT [*Whispers*].   Pierrette!   Pierrette!

PRUNELLA.   It is I, Pierrot!

PIERROT. Living or dead, which art thou?

PRUNELLA.   Wouldst thou know,
   Draw near and see!

[*A pause.* PIERROT *tries to advance, but fails.*

PIERROT.   Pierrette, my feet are slow
   For very shame: better on knees to go.

                          [*He kneels.*

   Now—if thou livest—for a sign stretch out
   Thy hand toward me!   Leave me not in doubt!

                    [*She remains motionless.*

   So, is it so?   To meet when parted most!
   Dead, thou art dead!   And there now stands thy
      ghost.

Alas, sweet ghost! what dost thou here with ACT III
   me,
Robbing the dead of thy dear company?
Go back where peace is; for no peace dwells
   here.

PRUNELLA. I stay with Love to look on thee, my
   dear.

PIERROT. Can death such pity to the dead be-
   queath?
I have no right of breath where thou dost
   breathe;
No cause to look on life, except thou see
The light of day which I destroyed for thee.

PRUNELLA. A little weeping, Pierrot, does not blind
The eyes of love.

PIERROT.   Ah me, too bitter kind,
Too ghostly gentle in thy speech thou art!
Peace be to thy sweet soul!

PRUNELLA.   Peace to thy heart!
Living or dead, I love thee.

PIERROT.   Say, then, why
Camest thou here? To tell me I must die?
Is it to-night?   [*Eagerly.*

PRUNELLA.   To-night were choice made free,
Wouldst thou give up thy life to come to
   me?

PIERROT. Yea, I will come. Yea, I will come!
                    [*He rises to his feet.*

PRUNELLA

Prunella. Beware!
>If you but touch me, all I am, you share
>For life, or death! So choose as you would
>be!
>
>Pierrot. I will do so. Yea, let the worms eat
>me,
>If now in that pure breast corruption eats!
>Thou smilest, am I dead?—It beats! It
>beats!
>
>Prunella. For thee, only for thee. Quick to thy
>nest,
>Thou weary wandering bird, and there take
>rest!
>
>> [Pierrot *drops his head on to her breast,
>> and sobs.*
>
>Nay, nay, lift up thy head, look not so ill!
>Earth is sweet under us, the stars shine still.
>Look how they number them! Look how they
>glow!
>
>Pierrot. It is for Pierrette—not for Pierrot!
>
>> [*Light begins to increase in the garden, and
>> the singing of birds is heard.*
>
>Prunella. Hush! hush! the birds are waking in
>the night;
>They sing of thee and me, and our delight!
>
>Pierrot. 'Tis not the birds: it is the stars that
>sing;
>Nay, not the stars, nor any mortal thing,

PRUNELLA

Either in earth beneath or heaven above;
The song thou hearest is the song of Love!
Hark! Look!

> [*They turn to the Statue, which is again flooded
> with light. Love's head is raised, and he
> plays upon his viol, while all the garden
> grows loud with song.*]

THE END

Printed by T. and A. Constable, Printers to His Majesty
at the Edinburgh University Press

Plays published by Sidgwick & Jackson, Ltd.

By LAURENCE HOUSMAN

THE CHINESE LANTERN. Pott 4to, 3s. 6d. net.

A fantastic play in a quaint Chinese setting, telling how Tikipu, the drudge of an art-school, tried to learn how to paint, and was taken away into a magic picture of Wiowani for three years. Meanwhile the little slave-girl Mee-Mee faithfully awaits his return, which occurs just as she has given up hope and is about to poison herself to avoid a forced marriage with Yunglangtsi, a gross body with a grocer's soul. Mee-Mee and Tikipu run away together.

PAINS AND PENALTIES: The Defence of Queen Caroline. Crown 8vo, cloth, 3s. 6d. net ; paper, 1s. 6d. net.

'This play has been censored. It is a play by a poet and artist. And it goes very deeply and hauntingly into the heart. The note that it sounds is the note of Justice, and he would indeed be either a fearful or a fawning reader who could find aught to object to in it.'—*Observer*.

By GRANVILLE BARKER

THE MARRYING OF ANN LEETE. *[Fourth Impression.*

THE VOYSEY INHERITANCE. *[Eighth Impression.*

WASTE. *[Eighth Impression.*

THE MADRAS HOUSE. *[Third Impression.*

Cloth, 2s. net each ; paper, 1s. 6d. net each.

The first three in one volume, 'Three Plays,' cloth, 5s. net.

'His plays are among the few that are worth seeing, and among the still fewer that are worth reading, and reading seriously and more than once.'—*Morning Post*.